Book 1
Windows 8 Tips for
Beginners
BY SAM KEY

&

Book 2
CSS Programming
Professional Made Easy
BY SAM KEY

Book 1
Windows 8 Tips for Beginners
BY SAM KEY

A Simple, Easy, and Efficient Guide to a Complex System of Windows 8!

Table Of Contents

Introduction

I want to thank you and congratulate you for purchasing the book, "Windows 8 Tips for Beginners: A Simple, easy, and efficient guide to a complex system of windows 8!"

This book contains proven steps and strategies on how to familiarize yourself with the new features of Windows 8 which were designed to make your computing experience simpler and more enjoyable. You will not only learn how to navigate through Windows 8 , but you will also learn how Windows 8 is similar to and different from the older versions so you can easily adjust and take advantage of the benefits that Windows 8 has in store for you.

Thanks again for purchasing this book, I hope you enjoy it!

Chapter 1: How is Windows 8 Different from Previous Versions?

With Windows 8, Microsoft launched a lot of new changes and features, some of which are minor , but others are major. Some of the changes you can see in Windows 8 are the redesigned interface, enhanced security and other online features.

Changes in the Interface

The most glaring change you will observe when you first open your computer with Windows 8 is that the screen looks completely different from older Windows versions. The Windows 8 interface has new features such as Start screen, hot corners, and live tiles.

•   The Start screen will be the main screen where you will find all of your installed programs and they will be in the form of "tiles". You can personalize your Start Screen by rearranging the tiles, selecting a background image and changing the color scheme.

•   You can navigate through Windows 8 using the "hot corners", which you activate by hovering the mouse pointer over the corners of the screen. For instance, if you want to switch to another open application, hover your mouse in the top-left corner of your screen and then click on the app.

•   Certain apps have Live Tile functions, which enable you to see information even if the app itself is not open. For instance, you can easily see the current weather on the Weather app tile from your Start screen; if you want to see more information, you can just click on the app to open it.

•   You can now find many of the settings of your computer in the Charms bar that you can open by hovering the mouse in the bottom-right or top-right corner of your computer screen.

Online Features in Windows 8

Because of the ease of accessing Internet now, many people have started to save their documents and other data online. Microsoft has made it easier to save on the cloud through their OneDrive service (this was formerly called SkyDrive). Windows 8 is capable of linking to OneDrive and other online social networks such as Twitter and Facebook in a seamless manner.

To connect your computer to OneDrive, sign in using your free Microsoft account instead of your own computer account. When you do this, all of the contacts, files and other information stored in your OneDrive are all in your Start screen. You can also use another computer to sign in to your Microsoft account and access all of your OneDrive files. You can also easily link your Flickr, Twitter and Facebook accounts to Windows 8 so you will be able to see the updates straight from your Start screen. You can also do this through the People app which is included in Windows 8.

Other Features

•   The Desktop is now simpler for enhanced speed. Yes, the Desktop is still included in Windows 8 and you can still manage your documents or open your installed programs through the Desktop. However, with Windows 8, a number of the transparency effects that frequently caused Windows Vista and Windows 7 to slow down are now gone. This allows the Desktop to operate smoother on nearly all computers.

•   The Start menu, once considered as a vital feature in previous Windows versions, is now the Start screen. You can now open your installed programs or search for your files through the Start screen. This can be quite disorienting if you are just starting with Windows 8.

•   Windows 8 has enhanced security because of its integrated antivirus program referred to as Windows Defender. This antivirus program is also useful in protecting you from different kinds of malware. In addition, it can aid in keeping you and your computer secure by telling you which data each of your installed apps can access. For instance, certain apps can access your location, so if you do not want other people to know where you are, just change your preference in the settings/configuration part of your apps.

How to Use Windows 8

Because Windows 8 is not like the older versions, it will possibly change how you have been using your computer. You may need quite some time to get accustomed to the new features, but you just need to remember that those changes are necessary to enhance your computing experience. For instance, if you have used older Windows versions, you may be used to clicking on the Start button to launch programs. You need to get used to using the Start screen with Windows 8. Of course, you can still use the Desktop view to make file and folder organization easier and to launch older programs.

You may need to switch between the Desktop view and the Start screen to work on your computer. Don't feel bad if you feel disoriented at first because you will get used to it. Moreover, if you just use your computer to surf the internet, you may be spending majority of your time in the Start screen anyway.

Chapter 2: How to Get Started with Windows 8

Windows 8 can truly be bewildering at the start because of the many changes done to the interface. You will need to learn effective navigation of both the Start screen and Desktop view. Even though the Desktop view appears similar to the older Windows versions, it has one major change that you need to get used to – the Start menu is no more.

In this chapter, you will learn how to work with the apps and effectively navigate Windows 8 using the Charms bar. You will learn where to look for the features that you could previously find in the Start menu.

How to Sign In

While setting up Windows 8, you will be required to create your own account name and password that you will use to sign in. You can also opt to create other account names and associate each account name with a specific Microsoft account. You will then see your own user account name and photo (if you have uploaded one). Key in your password and press enter. To select another user, click on the back arrow to choose from the available options. After you have signed in, the Start screen will be displayed.

How to Navigate Windows 8

You can use the following ways to navigate your way through Windows 8

•   You can use the hot corners to navigate through Windows 8. You can use them whether you are in the Desktop view or in the Start screen. Simply hover your mouse in the corner of the screen to access the hot corners. You will see a tile or a toolbar that you can then click to open. All the corners perform various tasks. For instance, hovering the pointer on the lower-left corner will return you to the Start screen. The upper-left corner will allow you to switch to the last application that you were using. The lower-right or upper-right corners gives you access to the Charms bar where you can either manage your printers or adjust the settings of your computer. Hover your mouse towards the upper-left corner and then move your mouse down to see the list of the different applications that you are simultaneously using. You can simply on any application to go back to it.

• You can also navigate through Windows 8 through different keyboard shortcuts.

o Alt+Tab is the most useful shortcut; you use it to switch between open applications in both the Start screen and Desktop view.

o You can use the Windows key to go back to the Start screen. It also works in both the Desktop view and Start screen.

o From the Start screen, you can go to the Desktop view by clicking on Windows+D.

• You can access the settings and other features of your computer through the toolbar referred to as Charms bar. Place your mouse pointer on the bottom-right or top-right corner of your screen to display the Charms bar wherein you can see the following icons or "charms":

o The Search charm allows you to look for files, apps or settings on your computer. However, a simpler method to do a search is through the Start screen wherein you can simply key in the name of the application or file that you want to find.

o You can think of the Share charm as a "copy and paste" attribute that is included in Windows 8 to make it easier for you to work with your computer. Using the Share charm, you can "copy" data like a web address or a picture from one app and then "paste" it onto another application. For instance, if you are reading a certain article in the Internet, you can share the website address in your Mail application so you can send it to a friend.

o The Start charm will allow you to go back to the Start screen. If you are currently on the Start screen, the Start charm will launch the latest app that you used.

○ The Devices charm displays all of the hardware devices that are linked to your computer such as monitors and printers.

○ Through the Settings charm, you can open both the general setting of your computer and the settings of the application that you are presently using. For instance, if you are presently using the web browser, you can access the Internet Options through the Settings charm.

How to Work with the Start Screen Applications

You may need to familiarize yourself with the Start screen applications because they are quite different from the "classic" Windows applications from previous versions. The apps in Windows 8 fill the whole screen rather than launching in a window. However, you can still do multi-tasking by launching two or more applications next to each other.

• To open an application from the Start screen, look for the app that you want to launch and click on it.

• To close an application hover your mouse at the top portion of the application, and you will notice that the cursor will become a hand icon, click and hold your mouse and then drag it towards the bottommost part of the screen and then release. When the app has closed, you will go back to the Start screen.

How to View Apps Side by Side

Even though the applications normally fill up the whole screen, Windows 8 still allows you to snap an application to the right or left side and then launch other applications beside it. For instance, you can work on a word document while viewing the calendar app. Here are the steps to view applications side by side:

1. Go to the Start screen and then click on the first app that you want to open.

2. Once the app is open, click on the title bar and drag the window to the left or right side of your computer screen.

3.   Release your mouse and you will see that the application has snapped to the side of your computer screen.

4.   You can go back to the Start screen by clicking at any empty space of the computer screen.

5.   Click on another application that you want to open.

6.   You will now see the applications displayed side by side. You can also adjust the size of the applications by dragging the bar.

Please note that the snapping feature is intended to work with a widescreen monitor. Your minimum screen resolution should be 1366 x 768 pixels to enjoy the snapping feature fully. If your monitor has a bigger screen, you will be able to snap more than two apps simultaneously.

How to cope with the Start menu

Many people have already complained about the missing Start menu in Windows 8. For many Windows users, the Start menu is a very vital feature because they use to open applications, look for files, launch the Control Panel and shut down their computer. You can actually do all of these things in Windows 8 too, but you will now have to look for them in different locations.

•   There are a number of ways to launch an application in Windows 8. You can launch an app by clicking the application icon on the taskbar or double-clicking the application shortcut form the Desktop view or clicking the application tile in the Start screen.

•   You can look for an app or a file by pressing the Windows key to go back to the Start screen. When you are there, you can simply key in the filename or app name that you want to look for. The results of your search will be immediately displayed underneath the search bar. You will also see a list of recommended web searches underneath the search results.

•   You can launch the Control Panel by going to the Desktop view and then hovering your mouse in the lower-right corner of the computer screen to display the Charms bar and then selecting Settings. From the Settings Pane, look for and choose Control Panel.

After the Control Panel pops up, you can start choosing your preferred settings.

•   You can shut down your computer by hovering the mouse in the lower-right corner of your screen to display the Charms bar and then selecting Settings. Click on the Power icon and then choose Shut Down.

Start Screen Options

If you prefer to continue working with the Desktop view more often, you actually have a number of alternatives that can let your computer operate more like the older Windows versions. One of these alternatives is the "boot your computer directly to the Desktop" rather than the Start screen. Here are the steps to change your Start screen options:

1.   Return to the Desktop view.

2.   Right-click the taskbar then choose Properties.

3.   You will then see a dialog box where you can choose the options that you want to change.

Chapter 3: How to Personalize Your Start Screen

If you are open to the idea of spending most of your time on the Start screen of your computer, there are different ways you can do to personalize it based on your preferences. You can change the background color and image, rearrange the applications, pin applications and create application groups.

•   You can change the background of your Start screen by hovering the mouse in the lower-right corner of your screen to open up the Charms bar and then selecting the Settings icon. Choose Personalize and then choose your preferred color scheme and background image.

•   You can change the lock screen picture by displaying the Charms bar again and the selecting the Settings icon. Choose Change PC settings and then choose Lock screen that is located near to the topmost part of the screen. Choose your preferred image from the thumbnail photos shown. You can also opt to click on Browse to choose your own photos. You will see the lock screen every time you return to your computer after leaving it inactive for a set number of minutes. However, you can also manually lock your screen by clicking on your account name and then choosing Lock.

•   You can change your own account photo by displaying the Charms bar and then choosing the Settings icon. Click on the Change PC setting and choose Account picture. You can look for your own photos by clicking Browse, will let you browse the folders in your computer. Once you find the picture you want to use, click on Choose image to set it as your account picture. If you are running a laptop, you can also use the built-in webcam to take a picture of yourself for your account photo.

How to Customize the Start Screen Applications

You do not really need to put up with the pre-arranged apps on your Start screen. You can change how they look by rearranging them based on your own preference. You can move an app by clicking, holding and dragging the application to your preferred location. Let go of your mouse and the app tile will automatically move to the new place.

You may also think that the animation in the live tiles is very disturbing while you are working. Do not worry because you can simply turn the animation off so that you will only see a plain background. You can do this by right-clicking the application that you wish to change. A toolbar pop up from the bottom part of your computer screen. Simply choose Turn live tile off and the animation if you don't want real-time notifications.

How to Pin Applications to the Start Screen

By default, you won't be able to see all of the installed applications on the Start screen. However, you can easily "pin" your favorite apps on the Start screen so you can access them easily. You can do this by clicking the arrow found in the bottom-left corner of your Start screen. You will then see the list of all the applications that you have installed. Look for the app you want to pin and the right-click it. You will see Pin to Start at the lowest part of the screen. Click on it to pin your app.

To unpin or remove an application from the Start screen, right-click the app icon you want to remove and then choose "Unpin from Start".

How to Create Application Groups

There are more ways to bring organization to your apps. One way is to create an app group wherein you can similar apps together. You can give a specific name for each app group for easier retrieval. You can create a new application group by clicking, holding and dragging an application to the right side until you see it on an empty space of the Start screen. Let go of your mouse to let the app be inside its own application group. You will be able to see a distinct space between the new app group that you have just created and the other app groups. You can then drag other apps into the new group.

You can name your new application group by right clicking any of the apps on the Start screen and then clicking Name group at the top of the application group. When choosing a group name, opt for shorter, but more descriptive names. After you have keyed in your group name, press the Enter key.

Chapter 4: How to Manage Your Files and Folders

The File Explorer found in the Desktop view is very handy in managing files and folders in your computer. If you are familiar with older Windows version, File Explorer is actually the same as Windows Explorer. You will usually use the File Explorer for opening, accessing and rearranging folders and files in the Desktop view. You can launch the File Explorer by clicking the folder icon found on the taskbar.

The View tab in the File Explorer enables you to alter how the files appear inside the folders. For instance, you may choose to the List view when viewing documents and the Large Icons view when looking at photos. You can change the content view by selecting the View tab and then choosing your preferred view from the Layout group.

For certain folders, you can also sort your files in different ways – by name, size, file type, date modified, date created, among others. You can sort your files by selecting the View tab, clicking on the Sort by button and then choosing your preferred view from the drop-down list.

How to Search Using the File Explorer

Aside from using the Charms bar to look for files, you can also use the Search bar in the File Explorer. Actually, the File Explorer provides search options that are more advanced than those offered by the Charms bar. This is very useful when you are finding it quite hard to look for a particular document.

Every time you key in a word into the search bar, you will see that the Search Tools tab automatically opens on the Ribbon. You can find the advanced search options on the Search Tools tab. You can use them to filter your search by size, file type or date modified. You can also see the latest searches that you have made.

How to Work with Libraries

Windows 8 has 4 main libraries: Documents, Music, Pictures and Videos. Whenever you need a specific file, you can search for them through the Libraries or groups of content that you can readily access via the File Explorer.

The folders and files that you create are not actually stored in the Libraries themselves. The libraries are just there to help you better organize your stuff. You can place your own folders inside the libraries without the need to change their actual location in your computer. For instance, you can place a folder your recent photos in the Pictures library and still keep the folder on your Desktop for ready access.

Libraries are particularly vital in Windows 8 since a lot of the applications on the Start screen such as Photos, Music and Vides use the libraries in looking for and displaying their content. For instance, all of the photos in your Pictures library are also in your Photos app.

You need to note that the applications on your Start screen are optimized for media so that it will be more trouble-free for you to watch videos, listen to music and view your pictures. The File Explorer is an essential tool in organizing your current media files into libraries so that you can easily enjoy them right from your Start screen.

The My Music, My Documents folders and other certain folders are automatically included in their own applicable libraries. But you can add your own folders to any of the Libraries by first locating the Folder you want to add and then right-clicking on it. Choose the Include in library and then choose your preferred library. This technique allows your folder to be both in your library and in its original location.

Chapter 5: How to Get Started with the Desktop

The Start screen really is a cool new feature of Windows 8. But if you will be doing more than surfing the internet, watching videos and listening to music, you need to familiarize yourself with the different features in the Desktop view.

How to Work with Files

The details of the File Explorer were already discussed in the previous chapter. In this chapter, you will learn how to open and delete files, navigate through the various folders, and more.

After you have opened the File Explorer and you instantly see the document that you wish to open, you can simply double-click on it to open it. But if you still need to go through the different folders, the Navigation pane is very useful in choosing a different folder or location.

How to Delete Files

 You can delete a file by clicking, holding and dragging the file directly to the Recycle Bin icon found on the Desktop. An easier way is choosing the file that you want to delete and then pressing the Delete key. Do not worry if you have unintentionally deleted a file. You can access the Recycle Bin to locate the deleted file and restore it to its original folder. You can do this by right-clicking the file that you want to restore and then choosing Restore.

But if you are certain that all files in the Recycle Bin can be permanently deleted, you can clear it by right-clicking the Recycle Bin icon and then choosing Empty Recycle bin.

How to Open an Application on the Desktop

You can do this by either clicking the application icon found on the taskbar or double-clicking the application shortcut found on the Desktop.

How to Pin Applications to the Taskbar

By default, only selected application icons will be included on your taskbar. But you can pin your most used application on the taskbar so you can readily access them. You can do this by right-clicking anyplace on the Start screen. You will then see a menu at the bottom of your screen. Choose the All apps button to show the list of all your installed applications. Look for the application you want to pin and the right-click it and then choose Pin to taskbar. You need to note, though, that you cannot pin all applications to your taskbar. There are certain applications that are designed to be launched from the Start screen only like Calendar and Messaging. Thus, you can only pin them to the Start screen.

How to Use Desktop Effects

Multi-tasking and working with several windows have become easier with Windows 8 because of the various Desktop effects now available to you.

•   You can use the Snap effect to quickly resize open windows. This is particularly useful when you are working with several windows simultaneously. You can use the Snap effect by clicking, holding and dragging a window to the right or the left until you see the cursor reach the edge of your screen. Release your mouse to snap the window into place. You can easily unsnap a window by clicking, dragging it down and then releasing your mouse.

•   Use the Peek effect for viewing the open windows from your taskbar. You can do this by hovering your mouse over any app icon on the taskbar that you want to view. You will then see a thumbnail preview of all open windows. You can view the full-sized window of the application by hovering the mouse over the app in the thumbnail preview.

•   Use the Shake feature for selecting a single window from a clutter of open windows and then minimizing the rest. You can do this by locating and selecting the window that you want to concentrate on. You can then gently shake the window back and forth to minimize the other open windows. When you shake the window once more, all of the windows that you minimized will get maximized again.

•   The Flip feature is useful in scrolling across a preview of all your open windows. You can also view any of the open applications on your Start screen using the Flip preview. The first three features – Snap, Shake and Peek – are for use only on the Desktop view. The Flip feature, on the other hand, can be used similarly in both the Desktop view and the Start screen. You can access the Flip preview by pressing and holding the Alt key and then pressing the Tab key. While you are still pressing the Alt key, press the Tab key to continue scrolling through your open windows. When you have spotted the application or the window that you want to view, stop pressing the Alt and Tab keys to display the app or window.

Conclusion

Thank you again for purchasing this book!

I hope this book was able to help you to use the new features of Windows 8.

The next step is to start personalizing your own Windows 8 so you can get the most out of it.

Finally, if you enjoyed this book, please take the time to share your thoughts and post a review on Amazon. We do our best to reach out to readers and provide the best value we can. Your positive review will help us achieve that. It'd be greatly appreciated!

Thank you and good luck!

Book 2
CSS Programming
Professional Made Easy
BY SAM KEY

Expert CSS Programming Language Success in a Day for any Computer User!

Table of Contents

Introduction

I want to thank you and congratulate you for purchasing the book, "Professional CSS Programming Made Easy: Expert CSS Programming Language Success In A Day for any Computer User!".

This book contains proven steps and strategies on how to effectively apply CSS style rules in making your webpages more appealing to your readers. In this book, the different aspects of CSS programming are discussed in simple language to make it easy for you to understand even if you have no previous experience in programming. In no time, you can start creating your own CSS style rules!

Thanks again for purchasing this book, I hope you enjoy it!

Chapter 1: What is CSS?

CSS is short for Cascading Style Sheets which is a simple design language that is meant to streamline the enhancement of web page presentations. Basically, through CSS, you will be able to manage how a web page looks and feels. When you use CSS, you will be able to control the background color or image in the web page, the color of the texts, the style of the font, the size of the columns, the column layout, the spacing in between paragraphs and a whole lot more of design effects.

Even though CSS is quite simple to understand, it can provide you with great control of how an HTML document is presented. People who study CSS often study other markup languages such as XHTML or HTML.

What are the advantages of CSS?

- CSS will allow you to save time. After you have written a CSS code once, you can then use the same sheet in various web pages. You can create a style for each web page element and then use it to as many HTML pages as you desire in the future.

- Your web pages will load faster. If you will use CSS in your web pages, you no longer have to write an HTML tag attribute all the time. You simple create 1 CSS rule of a tag and then use it for all the incidences of that specific tag. When you use less HTML codes, it translates to faster download speed.

- Your web pages become easier to maintain. If you wish to create a global change in your website, all you need to do is adjust the style and then all the elements included in your different web pages will be automatically adjusted.

- You will be able to enjoy better styles compared to HTML. The style attributes available for HTML codes are lesser compared to what you can work with when you use CSS. This means that you will be able to create top quality styles for your web pages.

- You will have multiple device compatibility. With CSS, you will be allowed to use content that can be optimized for different types of device. Even when you use the same HTML document, you can present the website in various versions for different devices such as mobile phones, tablets, desktop and even printing.

- You will be able to adopt web standards that are recognized globally. More and more people are losing interest in using HTML attributes and have started to recommend the use of CSS.

- You get to future-proof. By using CSS in your web pages now, you can also ensure that they will have compatibility with future browsers.

Creation and Maintenance of CSS

Only a small group of people within the World Wide Web Consortium (W3C) referred to as the CSS Working Group is allowed to create and maintain CSS. This group generates the CSS specifications which are then submitted to the W3C members for discussion and ratification. Only ratified specifications are given the recommendation signal by the W3C. You need to note that they are referred to as recommendations since the W3C cannot really dictate how the language is to be actually implementation. The software the implement the CSS language is created by independent organizations and companies.

Note: If you wish to know, yes, the W3C is the group that provides the recommendations on how the Internet should work and how it should progress.

Different CSS Versions

The W3C released CSS1 or Cascading Style Sheets Level 1was released as a recommendation in 1996. The recommendation included a description of the CSS together with a basic visual formatting model that can be used for every HTML tag.

In May 1998, the W3C released the recommendation for CSS2 or Cascading Style Sheets Level 2 which included further information that builds on CSS1. CSS2 added support for style sheets for specific media such as aural devices, printers, element tables and positioning and downloadable fonts.

Chapter 2: Various Types of CSS Selectors

A CSS is composed of different style rules that are translated by the browser for them to be applied to the specific elements in your web page. A style rule is further composed of 3 parts: selector, property and value. A selector is the HTML tag wherein the style rule will be applied. Examples include <table> or <h1>. A property is the specific attribute type that an HTML tag has. In simple terms, you could say that each HTML attribute is ultimately translated to a CSS property. Examples of properties include border or color. Values, on the other hand, are directly assigned to the properties. For instance, for the color property, you can assign a value of #000000 or black.

One way to write a CSS Style Rule Syntax is: Selector (property: value)

Ex. You can write the syntax rule for a table border as: table (border: 2px solid #C00;). The selector in this example is table while the property is the border. The specific value given for the property is 2px solid #C00.

In this chapter, we will be talking about the different kinds of selectors.

Type Selector

The selector in the example given above (table) is categorized under the Type Selector. Another example of a type Selector is "level 1 heading" or "h1). We can write a CSS Style Rule Syntax as: h1 (color: #36CFFF;). The selector in this example is h1 while the property is the color. The specific value given for the property is #36CFFF.

Universal Selector

This is designated by an asterisk (*) which means that the style rule syntax that you want to create will be applied to all elements in your webpage and not only to specific elements.

Example: *(color: #FFFFFF;). This style rule means that you want all of the elements (including fonts, borders, etc.) in your webpage to be white.

Descendant Selector

You use the descendant selector when you wish to apply a certain style rule for a specific element that lies within a specific element.

Example: ul em (color:#FFFFFF;), the value #FFFFFF (white) will only be applied to the property (color) if the selector/property <em> lies within the selector <ul>.

Class Selector

Using the Class Selector, you will be able to define a specific style rule that can be applied based on the specific class attribute of elements. This means that all of the elements that have that specific class attributed will have the same formatting as specified in the style rule.

Example 1: .white (color: #FFFFFF;). Here the class attribute is "white" and it means that the color "white" will be applied to all of the elements given the class attribute "white" in your document.

Example 2: h1.white (color: #FFFFFF;). This style rule is more specific. The class attribute is still "white" and the style rule will be applied to the elements given the class attribute "white" but ONLY if they are ALSO an <h1> or "level 1 heading" element.

You can actually give one or more class selectors for each element. For example, you can give the class selectors "center" and "bold" to a paragraph <p> by writing it as <p class="center,bold">.

ID Selector

You use an ID selector to create a style rule that is based on the specific ID attribute of the element. This means that all of the elements that have that specific ID will have the same format as defined in the style rule.

Example 1: #white (color: #FFFFFF;). The ID assigned here is "white" and the style rule means that all elements with the "white" ID attribute will be rendered black in your document.

Example 2: h1#white (color: #FFFFFF;). This is more specific because it means that the style rule will only be applied to elements with the ID attribute "white" ONLY IF they are a level 1 heading element.

The ID selectors are ideally used as foundations for descendant selectors. Example: #white h3 (color: #FFFFFF;). The style rule dictates that all level 3 headings located in the different pages of your website will be displayed in white color ONLY IF those level 3 headings are within tags that have an ID attribute of "white".

Child Selector

The Child Selector is quite similar to the Descendant Selector except that they have different functionalities.

Example: body > p (color: #FFFFFF;). The style rule states that a paragraph will be rendered in white if it is a direct child of the <body> element. If the paragraph is within other elements such as <td> or <div>, the style rule will not apply to it.

Attribute Selector

You can apply specific styles to your webpage elements that have specific attributes.

Example: input(type="text"](color: #FFFFFF;).

One benefit of the above example is that the specified color in the style rule will only affect your desired text field and will not affect the <input type="submit"/>.

You need to keep the following rules in mind when using attribute selectors:

• p[lang]. All elements of the paragraph that has a "lang" attribute will be selected.

- p[lang="fr"]. All elements of the paragraph that has a "lang" attribute AND the value "fr" in the "lang" attribute will be selected. Note that the value should exactly be "fr".

- p[lang~="fr"]. All elements of the paragraph that has a "lang" attribute AND CONTAINS the value "fr" in the "lang" attribute will be selected.

- p[lang |="ne"]. All elements of the paragraph that has a "lang" attribute AND CONTAINS value that is EITHER exactly "en" or starts with "en-" in the "lang" attribute will be selected.

Multiple Style Rules

It is possible for you to create multiple style rules for one specific element. The style rules can be defined in such a way that different properties are combined into a single block and specific values are assigned to each property.

Example 1:

h1(color: #35C; font-weight: bold; letter-spacing: .5em; margin-bottom: 1em; text-transform: uppercase;)

You will note that the properties and their corresponding values are separated from other property/value pairs by using a semi-colon. You can opt to write the combine style rules as a single line similar to the example above or as multiple lines for better readability. The example below is just the same as Example 1:

Example 2:

h1 (

color: #35C;

font-weight: bold;

letter-spacing: .5em;

margin-bottom: 1em;

text-transform: uppercase;

)

How to Group Selectors

You can actually apply one single style to different selectors. All you really need to do is write all the selectors at the start of your style rule but make sure that they are separated by a comma. The examples above both pertain to the selector or property "level 1 heading". If you want to apply the same style rule to "level 2 heading" and "level 3 heading", you can include h2 and h3 in the first line, as follows:

Example:

h1, h2, h3 (

color: #35C;

font-weight: bold;

letter-spacing: .5em;

margin-bottom: 1em;

text-transform: uppercase;

)

Note that the sequence of the selector element is not relevant. You can write it as h3,h2,h1 and the style rule will exactly be the same. It means that the specified style rules will still be applied to all the elements of the selectors.

It is also possible to create a style rule that combines different class selectors.

Example:

#supplement, #footer, #content (

position: absolute;

left: 520px;

width: 210px;

)

Chapter 3: Methods of Associating Styles

There are actually 4 methods of associating styles within an HTML document – Embedded CSS, Inline CSS, External CSS and Imported CSS. But the two most frequently used are Inline CSS and External CSS.

Embedded CSS

This method uses the <style> element wherein the tags are positioned within the <head>...</head> tags. All elements that exist within your document will be affected by a rule that has been written using this syntax. The generic syntax is as follows:

<head>

<style type="text/css" media="...">

Style Rules

. . . .

</style>

</head>

The following attributes that are connected to the <style> element are as follows:

•   Type with value "text/css". This attribute indicates the style sheet language as a content-type (MIME type). You need to note that this attribute is always required.

•   Media with values as "screen", "tty", "tv", "projection", "handheld", "print", "braille", "aural" or "all". This attribute indicates what kind of device the webpage will be shown. This attribute is only optional and it always has "all" as a default value.

 Example:

```
<head>

<style type="text/css" media="screen">

h2(

color: #38C;

)

</style>

</head>
```

Inline CSS

This method uses the style attribute of a specific HTML element in defining the style rule. This means that the style rule will only be applied to the specific HTML element ONLY. The generic syntax is as follows: <element style="...style rules....">

Only one attribute is connected to the <style> attribute and it is as follows:

•   Style with value "style rules". The value that you will specify for the style attribute is basically a combination of various style declarations. You should use a semicolon to separate the different style declarations.

Example:

<h2 style ="color:#000;">. This is inline CSS </h2>

External CSS

This method uses the <link> element in defining the style rule. You can use it to add external style sheets within your webpage. The external style sheet that you will add will have a different text file that has the extension .css. All the style rules that you want to apply to your webpage elements will be added inside the external text file and then you can append the text file in any of your web pages by creating the <link> element. The general syntax that you will be using will be:

<head>

<link type="text/css" href=" ..." media=" ..." />

</head>

The following attributes that are connected with the <style> elements are as follows:

•   Type with the value "text/css". This indicates that you are using a MIME type or a content type for your style sheet language. Note that you are always required to use this attribute.

•   Href with value "URL". This attribute will indicate the specific style sheet file that contains your style rules. Again, you are also always required to use this attribute.

•   Media with value "screen", "tty", "tv", "projection", "handheld", "print", "braille", "aural" or "all". This attribute indicates the specific media device that you will use to display the document. This attribute is only optional and it has a default value of "all".

Example wherein the style sheet file is named as docstyle.css:

h2, h3 (

color: #38C;

font-weight: bold;

letter-spacing: .5em;

margin-bottom: 2em;

text-transform: uppercase;

)

Then you can add your style sheet file "docstyle.css" in your webpage by adding these rules:

<head>

<link type="text/css" href="docstyle.css" media="all" />

</head>

Imported CSS

This method which uses the @import rule is the same as the <link> element because it is used to import an external style sheet file to your webpage. The generic syntax of this method is as follows:

<head>

<@import "URL";

</head>

Here is another alternative syntax that you can use:

<head>

<@import url ("URL");

</head>

Example:

<head>

@import "docstyle.css'"

</head>

How to Override CSS Style Rules

The following can override the style rules that you have created using the above four methods:

•   An inline style sheet is given the number one priority. This means that an inline style sheet will always supersede a rule that has been written with a <style>...</style> tag or a rule that has been defined in an external stylesheet file.

• 	A rule that has been written with a <style>...</style> tag will always supersede a style rule that has been defined in an external stylesheet file.

• 	The rules that you define within an external stylesheet file is always given the lowest priority. This means that any rules defined within the external file will only be applied if the 2 rules above aren't valid.

How to Handle an Old Browser:

Currently, there are a lot of old browsers that are not yet capable of supporting CSS. When you are working with these kind of browsers, you need to write your embedded CSS within the HTML document. Here is an example on how you can embed CSS in an old browser:

<style type="text/css">

<!—

Body, td (

    Color: red;

)

-->

</style>

How to Add a CSS Comment

In case it is necessary for you to include an additional comment within the style sheet block, you can easily do this by writing your comment within /*....this is a comment in style sheet....*/. The /*....*/ method used in C++ and C programming languages can also be used in adding comments in a multi-line block.

Example:

/* This is an external style sheet file */

```
h3, h2, h1 (

color: #38C;

font-weight: bold;

letter-spacing: .5em;

margin-bottom: 2em;

text-transform: uppercase;

)
/* end of style rules. */
```

Chapter 4: Measurement Units

There are several measurements that CSS can support. These include absolute units like inch, centimeter, points, etc. They also include relative measures like em unit and percentage. These values are important when you want to specify the different measurements you want to include in your style rule. Example:

border="2px solid black".

Here are the most common measurements that you will use in creating CSS style rules:

Unit of Measure	Description	Example
%	Indicates measurements as a percentage in relation to another value which is normally an enclosing element	p {font-size: 12pt; line-height: 150%;}
cm	Indicates measurements in centimeter	div {margin-bottom: 1.5cm;}
em	A relative number used in measuring font height using em spaces. One em unit is equal to the size of a particular font. This means, if you want a certain font to have a size of 10pt, one "em" unit is equal to 10pt and 3em is equal to 30pt.	p {letter-spacing: 6em;}
ex	A number used to define a measurement in relation to the x-height of a font. The x-height is defined by the height of letter x in lowercase in any	p {font-size: 20pt: line-height: 2ex;}

	given font.	
in	Indicates measurements in inches	p {word-spacing: .12in;}
mm	Indicates measurements in millimeter	p {word-spacing: 12mm;}
pc	Indicates measurements in picas. One pica is equal to 12 points. This means that there are six picas in one inch.	p {font-size: 18pc;}
pt	Indicates measurements in points. One point is equal to 1/72 of one inch.	body {font-size: 20pt;}
px	Indicates measurements in screen pixel	p {padding: 32px;}

Chapter 5: Style Rules Using Colors

A color in CSS style rules is indicated by color values. Normally, the color values are used to define the color of either the background of an element or its foreground (that is, its text). You can also utilize colors to change how your borders and other aesthetic effects look.

Color values in CSS rules can be specified using the following formats:

• Hex code using the syntax #RRGGBB. Example: p {color: #FFFF00;}. The six digits represent one specific color wherein RR represents the value for red, GG the value for green and BB the value for blue. You can get the hexadecimal values of different colors from graphics software such as Jasc Paintshop Pro and Adobe Photoshop. You can also use the Advanced Paint Brush to get the hexadecimal values. You need to note that the six digits should always be preceded by the hash or pound sign (#).

• Short hex code using the syntax #RGB. Example: p {color: #7A6;}. This is the shorter version of the hexadecimal value. You can also get them from Jasc Paintshop Pro, Adobe Photoshop or Advanced Paint Brush.

• RGB % using the syntax rgb (rrr%, ggg%, bbb%). Example: p{color: rgb (40%, 50%, 40%);}. This format is actually advisable to use because not all browsers support this type of format.

• RGB Absolute using the syntax rgb (rrr,ggg, bbb). Example: p {color: rgb (255,0,0);}

• Keyword using the syntax black, aqua, etc. Example: p {color: red;}

Chapter 6: How to Set Backgrounds

What you will learn in this chapter includes how to define the background of the different elements in your web page. You can use any of the following background properties for specific elements in your webpage:

•   You can use the background color property to define the background color of your element.

•   You can use the background image property to define the background image of your element.

•   You can use the background repeat property to control whether your background image will be repeated or not.

•   You can use the background position property to control the position of the background image.

•   You can use the background attachment property to define whether your image is fixed or will scroll with the rest of the webpage.

•   You can use the background property to combine the above properties into one style rule.

Background Color

Here is a sample of how you can define the background color:

RED

This will result in RED.

Background Image

Here is a sample of how you can define the background image:

<table style="background-image:url (/images/pattern1.jpg);">

<tr><td>

The table now has an image in the background.

</td></tr>

</table>

How to Repeat a Background Image

In case your image is small, you can opt to repeat your background image. Otherwise, you can simple utilize the "no-repeat" value in the background-repeat property if you do not wish to have your background image repeated. This means that your image will only be displayed once. Note that "repeat value" is the default value in the background-repeat property.

Example:

<table style="background-image:url (/images/pattern2.jpg);

        background-repeat: repeat;">

<tr><td>

The background image in this table will be repeated several times.

</td></tr>

</table>

Here is a sample rule if you want the background image to be repeated vertically:

<table style="background-image:url (/images/pattern2.jpg);

        background-repeat: repeat-y;">

<tr><td>

The background image in this table will be repeated vertically.

</td></tr>

</table>

Here is a sample rule if you want the background image to be repeated horizontally:

<table style="background-image:url (/images/pattern2.jpg);

            background-repeat: repeat-x;">

<tr><td>

The background image in this table will be repeated horizontally.

</td></tr>

</table>

How to Set the Position of the Background Image

Here is a sample of how you can define the position of a background image at 150 pixels from the left side:

<table style="background-image: url (/images/pattern2.jpg);

            Background-position:150px;">

<tr><td>

The position of the background is now 150 pixels from the left side.

</td></tr>

</table>

Here is a sample of how you can define the position of a background image at 300 pixels from the top and 150 pixels from the left side:

Background-position:150px 300px;">

<tr><td>

The position of the background is now 300 pixels from the top and 150 pixels from the left side.

</td></tr>

</table>

How to Define the Background Attachment

The background attachment indicates whether the background image that you have set is fixed in its place or scrolls when you move the webpage.

Here is an example on how to write a style rule with a background image that is fixed:

<p style="background-image:url (/images/pattern2.jpg);

        Background-attachment:fixed;">

The paragraph now has a background image that is fixed.

</p>

Here is an example on how to write a style rule with a background image that scrolls with the webpage:

<p style="background-image:url (/images/pattern2.jpg);

        Background-attachment:scroll;">

The paragraph now has a background image that scrolls with the webpage.

</p>

How to Use the Shorthand Property

You can actually utilize the background property in order to define all of the background properties all at the same time.

Example:

The background image of this paragraph has a scroll and repeated properties.

Chapter 7: How to Set Font Properties

What you will learn in this chapter includes how to define the following font properties to a specific element in your webpage:

•   You can use the font family property to adjust the face of your selected font.

•   You can use the font style property to make your fonts either oblique or italic.

•   You can use the font variant property to include the "small caps" effect in your fonts.

•   You can use the font weight property to decrease or increase how light or bold your fonts are displayed.

•   You can use the font size property to decrease or increase the sizes of your fonts.

•   You can use the font property to define a combination of the font properties above.

How to Define the Font Family

Here is an example on how you can define the font family of a specific element. As value of the property, you can use any of the font family names available:

This message is displayed either in calibri, arial or the default serif font. It will depend on the existing fonts in your system.

How to Define the Font Style

Here is an example on how you can define the font style of a specific element. The values that you can use are oblique, italic or normal.

This message is displayed in oblique style.

How to Define the Font Variant

Here is an example on how you define the font variant of a specific element. The values that you can use are small-caps or normal.

This message is displayed in normal font variant.

How to Define the Font Weight

Here is an example on how you can define the font weight of a specific element. With this property, you will be able to define how bold you want your fonts to be. The values that you can use are bold, normal, lighter, bolder, 100, 200, 300, 400, 500, 600, 700, 800, and 900.

The font is displayed with normal font weight.

The font is displayed with lighter font weight.

The font is displayed with 800 font weight.

How to Define the Font Size

Here is an example on how you can define the font size of a specific element. With this property, you will be able to control the font sizes in your webpage. The values that you can use include small, medium, large, x-small, xx-small, xx-large, x-large, larger, smaller, size in % or size in pixels.

The font is displayed with 18 pixels font size.

The font is displayed with large font size.

The font is displayed with larger font size.

How to Define the Font Size Adjust

Here is an example on how you can define the font size adjust of a specific element. With this property, you will be able to adjust the x-height in order to make the legibility of your fonts better. The values that you can use include any number.

The font is displayed with 0.75 font size adjust value.

How to Define the Font Stretch

Here is an example on how you can define the font stretch of a specific element. With this property, you can allow the computer of your webpage readers to have a condensed or expanded version of the font you have defined in your elements. The values that you can use include normal, narrower, wider, condensed, extra-condensed, semi-condensed, ultra-condensed, semi-expanded, ultra-expanded, expanded and extra-expanded

If this does not seem to work, it is probably that the computer you are using does not have an expanded or condensed version of the font that was used.

How to Use the Shorthand Property

You can utilize the font property to define the font properties all at the same time.

Example:

This applies all of the defined properties on the text all at the same time.

Conclusion

Thank you again for purchasing this book!

I hope this book was able to help you to understand the basic CSS styling rules.

The next step is to apply what you have just learned in your own webpage.

Finally, if you enjoyed this book, please take the time to share your thoughts and post a review on Amazon. We do our best to reach out to readers and provide the best value we can. Your positive review will help us achieve that. It'd be greatly appreciated!

Thank you and good luck!

Check Out My Other Books

Below you'll find some of my other popular books that are popular on Amazon and Kindle as well. Simply click on the links below to check them out. Alternatively, you can visit my author page on Amazon to see other work done by me.

Android Programming in a Day

Python Programming in a Day

C Programming Success in a Day

C Programming Professional Made Easy

JavaScript Programming Made Easy

PHP Programming Professional Made Easy

C ++ Programming Success in a Day

Windows 8 Tips for Beginners

HTML Professional Programming Made Easy

If the links do not work, for whatever reason, you can simply search for these titles on the Amazon website to find them.